M000036363

The Reluctant Seal

*The journey one man took to find his soul. During the
journey he found self-awareness. He learned how to forgive
others but most importantly he learned how to forgive himself!*

Ken LaBelle

The Reluctant Seal

ACKNOWLEDGEMENTS

I would like to thank the many angels, sent from God, who helped me to come to grips with my past. These angels have helped be greatly along this journey. They include the many people that read and helped me assemble this book.

My publisher Jacquetta Dantzler and Live on Purpose Publishing for all of their support and hard work in making this book a reality.

Chris LaBelle and Chris Pollard. Who helped me deal with the conflict that raged in me and helped me put my history into a helpful prospective. These two both asked me the same questions 10 years apart. Their question was "If you were asked to do it again, knowing what you know now would you do anything differently?"

My loving wife Stephanie who continues to remind me of my three questions and is one of the biggest blessings my Lord has ever given me.

Several unnamed veterans I have been blessed to talk with at different Veteran Hospitals along this journey.

CONTENTS

Final Inspection

By Joshua Helterbran

The soldier stood and faced his God,

Which must always come to pass;

He hoped his shoes were shining bright,

Just as brightly as his brass.

"Step forward now, soldier,

How shall I deal with you?

Have you turned the other cheek?

To my church have you been true?"

The soldier squared his shoulders and said,

"No, Lord, I guess I ain't;

Because those of us who carry guns,

Can't always be a saint.

I've had to work most Sundays,

And at times my talk was rough;

I've had to break your rules my Lord,

Because the world is awfully tough.

But, I never took a thing

That wasn't mine to keep;

Though I worked a lot of overtime,

When the bills got just too steep.

And I never passed a cry for help,

Though at times I shook with fear;

And sometimes ... God forgive me,

I've wept unmanly tears.

I know I don't deserve a place

Among the people here;

They never wanted me around,

Except to calm their fears.

If you've a place for me here, Lord,

It needn't be so grand;

I never expected or had too much,

But if you don't, I'll understand."

There was a silence all around the throne,

Where the saints often trod;

As the soldier waited quietly,

For the judgment of his God.

"Step forward now, soldier,

You've borne your burdens well;

Come walk peacefully on Heaven's streets,

You've done your time in HELL!"

1 INTRO

For over 40 years I have had violent, recurring nightmares. These nightmares wake me from my sleep. When I awake, I keep small fragments of the memory that caused the nightmare. I can remember brief moments of what the dream was about. Most of the nightmares were inspired by the same event. They often appeared to be in the same place and period of time. The dreams often cause me to awaken by violently jumping out of bed. I am awakened as if ready to, or already engaged in a fight. At other times they just startled me awake.

I know some of the things that almost always cause one of these nightmares. Those triggers can be directly related to things going on in my life. One of the things I know of is when I try to develop or maintain a physically disciplined lifestyle. By that, I mean getting into a strenuous workout routine where I begin working out daily. Another trigger is trying to remember or discuss my dreams or experiences. The final thing that almost always triggers nightmares is realistic violent war movies. Avoiding these known triggers helps but at other times there seems to be no rhyme or reason for the dreams.

I have always had two different memories of my military time. This does not make much sense to me and at times, has caused real conflict in my life. I mean, how can I have two very different memories during the same period of my life? These memories are in stark contrast to each other. At times one memory seems more real than the other. Both of the memories have very specific detailed information. I have struggled to understand these conflicting memories and how they relate to my nightmares for many years.

There are times that my SEAL memories do not seem real. I mean they appear to be made up. Then I get asked a question about some aspect of being a SEAL that I could only know if I had been there and done that. At other times I cannot recall simple details of SEAL training. It is this conflict of firsthand knowledge that causes a great struggle within me. It really bothers me that I have memories that do not always align with each other. How can I have been in two places at the same time? I mean only crazy people have more than one memory about the same event, right?

Before writing this, I had only described these memories to a few people. And never in great detail. I would have nightmares for several days after discussing the memories. Also, I lack a lot of detail. The people I would discuss this with vary. All of the people I have ever talked to have one thing in common, they were also veterans. It took me many years to gain enough confidence to talk about these memories and my ongoing struggle. Because I believed only crazy people have conflicting memories, right? These veterans I happened to talk to all were in specialized military training. The most common explanation they had for my dual memory was that I was either heavily debriefed or I'm nuts.

One day I was walking into the Veterans Administration Hospital for a "Serviced Connected Disability" appointment and I accidentally walked into a counselor's office. After I apologized for intruding, the counselor asked me what was wrong. I told her the name of the doctor I was looking for. She repeated her question of what was wrong. I told her that nothing was wrong I was just in the wrong place. She repeated her question. I repeated my answer that nothing was wrong.

She told me that, in her practice, she has seen a lot of veterans like myself. She had seen enough to recognize when something was bothering them. After her strong insistence that something was wrong and several more denials on my part, I spoke up, in detail, for the first time in my life. I described the emotional conflict that had been raging in me.

As my family will tell you I am not a person that shows much emotion. Ok, I show anger a lot but not many other emotions. But as I was speaking to this counselor I could not hold back the tears. I explained the memory conflict I had been having. How could both of my memories exist during the same period of my life? Am I crazy? Am I insane? Am I delusional?

We spoke for a while and I explained the history of my nightmares and the continuing conflict that my memories were causing. She suggested that what I had been through was more than likely a major debriefing and I was suffering from Post-Traumatic Stress Disorder.

However, she said that she was not my counselor and could not be sure. She said she had seen enough veterans to make the statement. She suggested I start writing in a journal the bits of the nightmare I could remember. I told her I do not journal, never have, and do not plan on starting one. In college, I lost points and my grades suffered because I would not keep a journal. Even at my church during Bible study, the instructors know that I will not keep a journal.

For some reason, this time when this stranger suggested it, I was inclined to try. At the time I could not have told you why. I now believe that my reason for agreeing to it was prompted by the Holy Spirit. Why else after all these years of others telling me to write things down, this time it just clicked. My guess is that there was a change in my spirit. As a side note for all of those people who suggested it before and I ignored your advice, I am truly sorry.

Looking back now, as I write this, I am surprised by my thoughts. Just before accidentally running into this person I was baptized, as a Christian, as an adult. This is the only explanation that makes sense to me. It is all a God thing. He intervened to answer my prayer and remove this conflict from my life. I know that to some this sounds hokey. But, it is from these notes that this story comes.

2 BEFORE

I suppose the best place to start is at the beginning. I grew up when the Vietnam War was going on and the protest against it was raging. Patriotism, to me, was on the decline. While people still seemed to hold the same core values, some of those values also seemed to be fading. The movement of the 1960s was growing and it seemed we were a country dividing.

My father was a Marine, which in and of itself is not too unique. He was a Marine Corps drill instructor for many years before he left the Marine Corps. His Marine Corps time, I now believe, shaped how he would raise his children, especially me. You see I was the middle child and the biggest. Being a typical blue-collar family, my dad worked many hours. Mom stayed home and took care of the chores around the house but Dad still took care of most of the discipline.

Like most boys my age, I was in Boy Scouts. As it happened I was fortunate to become very good friends with the scoutmaster's son. I could be found tagging along with him as we worked our way up to Eagle. I do not remember much involvement from my parents during my childhood. I don't say that with a "poor me" attitude because I've never felt that way. I say it because as a middle child my parents had stuff going with the other four kids. My scouting actions did not require their attention because I had an adult watching over me that they knew and trusted.

During high school, I was on the swim team. I swam the maximum number of events allowed, three. While I was not exceptional, I did alright. Last I knew, my record in the 50-yard freestyle at my high school still stands 35 years later. It helps that the school's pool closed three years after I graduated.

While in high school I was a social outcast. This was partly because of my upbringing. I had developed an exceptional sense of fair play. You see I didn't fit in with any particular group during high school. I was mostly on the outside looking in. I didn't fit in with the bright kids because I wasn't considered smart enough. I didn't fit in with the jocks because swimming wasn't considered a sport. I didn't fit in with the rowdier elements because I didn't take to ganging up on individuals. The way I was taught if I have a problem with somebody, you take that problem to them. If I needed more than myself to fix this problem then it is not the other person's problem it is mine.

Because of my strong sense of fair play, when I saw unbalanced fights I would always jump in with the underdog or the smaller sized group. This attitude didn't sit well with any of the club groups or bullies. But it did teach me to fight.

I did get high marks in many advanced classes. This was not because of my academic abilities, it was because I had two advantages: One,

I was working as an apprentice photographer and two, I was blessed with an understanding of all things mechanical. It was during my first year in high school that my algebra teacher approached me and asked me if I wanted an "A" in his class. Of course I responded "yes". My requirement to get an "A" was to take pictures at his daughter's wedding. He would supply the film, I would take the pictures and he would have them developed. So for a Saturday afternoon, I could receive an "A" in his class for that semester. That was a real no-brainer. This allowed me to pursue an extra hour of auto shop during his class period.

The auto shop instructor merely asked for me to provide a note from my algebra instructor that I could work on cars during that period, which he was happy to provide. Shortly afterward, one of my science instructors offered me a similar deal for his class, at which point, of course, I said yes. I was to work on his wife's car during his science class, and in exchange, I would receive an "A".

That was pretty much how I graduated high school with honors. I believe there were only three or four classes in high school that I actually attended other than auto shop and photography. Thanks to those teachers I was able to graduate with honors never having attended any of those challenging classes.

After high school, I continued living in a large manufacturing area. I naturally assumed that I would go to work in one of the factories. The year I graduated was the first year that the main employer moved all testing for skilled trades to one location. Before this change, each plant did its own testing and selection for skilled trade apprentices. I was looking for something more than a job working on the assembly line. So I applied for skilled trades since I was pretty good with my hands. I was accepted and allowed to test for a skilled trade job.

Ironically when they gave me the test results I had the highest overall score. Because of affirmative action requirements, I was told I would never get a job. Let alone a job in skilled trades. The military draft had recently ended making the military an all-volunteer organization. So I left that interview and joined the Navy. People asked me why the Navy. I like camping. I heard my dad's friends who were in the Army or the Marine Corps complain about always sleeping in the mud and how they did not like camping after they got out. After that, I didn't want to join the Army or the Marine Corps.

That left the Air Force or the Navy. The Air Force would not offer or guarantee a position and/or training that would equate to a civilian skilled trade job. The Navy would. So, the way I figured it, the Navy was the way to go. Also, I should always have a dry place to sleep - so I joined the Navy.

Before leaving for boot camp my father sat me down and offered me two pieces of advice. The first was don't volunteer for anything. The second was to find something, anything and be the very best at it. He said by being the very best at something, you could get yourself out of tight spots if you get into trouble.

So off to boot camp I went. There's something about the Great Lakes Naval Station in January that just takes your breath away. That would likely be the extremely cold air that you have to breathe whenever you are outside exercising. While in boot camp I was made part of the honor guard. I was the tallest at 6 foot 6 inches and I was placed in the center of the flag detail. This was a huge advantage. Being part of the honor guard meant we went to every ceremony and every graduation at the base. This detail got us out of some of the more mundane training that others enjoy during boot camp. Standing at attention, and standing still for all this time was something my parents never thought they would see. Many years later, I would find out that my graduation from boot camp and being an honor guard was the proudest moment of my father's life.

After boot camp, I went to the engineering training school that I was guaranteed at my enlistment. I went to Boiler Operators Class A School. This turned out to be more of an advantage to me than I ever thought at the time. After graduating from A school I had earned the rank of firemen (E3). Don't laugh, it beats being called a seaman. It also gave me a significant pay raise. After school, it was off to the fleet.

So after a brief stop at home, I was off to Rota Spain to join the "regular Navy." When I got to my ship, I was escorted to check in with the lead petty officer for the boiler operator in crew quarters. I asked for the person I needed to check in with and found him in a poker game. He had a pair of 2s and another guy had a full house. As I watch this first-class petty officer bluff this young kid out of the pot, I was surprised, to say the least. After the hand, I presented him my orders and asked him if this is an open game. He asked what division I was going into. I told him I was a boiler technician, he told me to sit down. So I tossed my seabag in the corner and they dealt me in.

I grew up playing cards. I would watch my dad play and as I got older I could sit in on hands. That day we played for several hours and I won several hundred dollars. Not too bad for not even being officially on board the ship yet.

After finishing the poker game, I did the check-in thing which included visiting the Chief Engineer Office, the Disbursement Office, and meeting the Captain of the ship. This was all pretty exciting as it was my first time doing anything like this. When you're in boot camp you are told where to go, told to stay as a group and you are treated like a piece of meat. As a matter of fact, that's what you were called, "a piece of meat." Now, in the fleet you were treated like a real person, what a difference.

I settled into ship life well. The normal at sea, shipboard routine consisted of four hours of duty watch followed by eight hours off. A watch for me was in one of the two boiler rooms. I started as what was call a messenger. My duty was to make rounds every fifteen minutes. A round was to check each piece of equipment and record the specific condition of each piece of equipment. The equipment consisted of fuel pumps, forced draft blowers, booster pumps, main feedwater pumps and critical areas of the high-pressure boilers.

Most ships from this period of time had three types of drives for the pumps: A hand drive, an electrical drive, and a steam turbine. The steam turbine is the drive that is used most during normal operation. The fuel pump supplied the boiler burners with the Navy distillment (in essence jet fuel). Some systems, like the water supply system, used more than one pump. A booster pump supplied water to the main feed pumps. The main feedwater pumps pumped feed water to the boilers. The booster pumps were electrical. The main feed pumps were a steam turbine. The backup feedwater pumps were steam or compressed air pumps. The forced draft blowers were steam turbine with an electrical backup blower. The hand pump was used when no electrical or steam power was available. The hand pump supplied the boiler burners with fuel until steam was made. "Making a round" meant going to each piece of equipment and recording on a log sheet the critical information. Critical information consisted of several bearing temperatures, input and output pressures, gland leakage, vibration levels, and general operating conditions.

After working as a messenger for only a few months, I was promoted to fireman. A fireman is a glorified way of saying, "stand in front of a really hot furnace and turn burners on and off as needed." A short while later I started training as a top watch. The top watch is the person who stands around and watches everything. The top watch is in charge of the fire room and is the person that is supposed to know what to do if anything goes wrong.

On my ship, we had a typical three-man crew to stand watch. A watch consisted of four hours working and eight hours off and we ran 24/7 while away from our home port. The reason we were allowed to run with such a small crew was because of the automatic controls on the boiler. The automatic controls did the job of two or three people. While working to be a top watch you also learned to do repairs on all of the supporting mechanical equipment that supplied the boiler. Through an unusual turn of events, the automatic controls broke. No one on board ship was authorized or had the security clearance to work on them.

3 BEGINNING

The Navy, in its infinite wisdom, had nobody around who was qualified to fix these controls. So consequently, we went from four hours on with eight hours off to the opposite, eight hours on with four hours off because all the controlling points had to be operated by hand. These controls maintained the proper water level in the boilers.

The boilers made steam, steam powered the turbines, turbines turned the machinery. The machinery could be a pump, blower, generator or even the ship engines. The boiler made the steam so that all the water was in the gas state of the steam. Too little water in the boiler and the boiler blows up. Too much water in the boiler, the water gets into the steam, the water hits the turbine, and turbine blows up. The controls also maintained the proper air in the boiler. Too much air and the fire could get blown out. Too little air could choke the fire out. Additionally, the location to manually operate these controls had no cooling air for the operator.

While speaking with the Division Chief and the Assistant Chief

Engineer, it was decided I could try to repair the equipment using the manuals. It was an interesting project. I was able to accomplish the repairs which meant I got all of the equipment back up and running. This allowed the ship's boiler operators to get back on a normal shift of four hours on eight hours off, plus I learned a new skill, win-win.

A few months later I was ordered to report to the Chief Engineer's office. There I learned that I was being temporarily transferred to the fleet maintenance group to go to school on the automatic combustion control equipment. I was told that it was an extremely difficult school. As it turned out, I was the lowest ranking individual in my class. After I completed and passed the school, I received certification for automatic combustion controls and returned to my ship. It was at this point I was told I had received a security clearance and told the responsibility that came with it. I arrived just in time to leave for a six-month deployment in the Mediterranean Sea.

Whenever I worked on combustion controls I had a pair of ultralight coveralls that I wore. These coveralls have no insignias to identify my rank. This was not by design the coveralls were the most moisture-wicking cooling things I had to wear. This type of repair work was often in the hottest areas of the ship. So anything that allowed me to cool down was welcome.

On our way across the Atlantic Ocean to the Mediterranean Sea, I was ordered to the Chief Engineer's office. In the Chief Engineer's office, I was told to get my coveralls on, pack a ditty bag (toiletries) and prepare for a helicopter transfer to another ship to work on their controls. I was being "loaned" out as it was explained to me.

I boarded the helicopter and flew to another ship in our fleet. When we landed on their flight deck, I stepped out of the helicopter, I was saluted by the Lieutenant Commander. If you are unfamiliar with boarding a ship, you salute the flag and the officer of the deck when getting on or getting off. Having never arrived on a ship by helicopter before, I assumed that this was protocol. I grabbed my gear and walked over to the Lieutenant Commander who said, "The captain will see you right away, Sir."

I was quite surprised at being called sir, as a Lieutenant Commander was much, much, much more senior in rank than I was. Sir means "senior in rank" and is a formal requirement when addressing a superior. In the Captain's quarters, the Captain asked me what I needed from the ship to perform the work I was to complete. As I did not know the work I was there to preform, I asked for clarification as to why I was there. I was informed that the automatic controls were not working. He was told I could make the repairs. As I was unfamiliar with the layout of his ship, I asked for someone from the boiler division. I requested a second class boiler operator who knew the ship and could be assigned to me while I was on board ship. I informed the captain that while this petty officer was working on the controls with me he should be off the duty roster. The reason for this is that sometimes repairs take 12, 13 or 14 hours straight before you can stop.

I was assigned an individual and we got started. As we got into the repairs the Petty Officer kept referring to me as sir. When I asked him why, he told me that, he was told, that an officer from the maintenance group was coming to fix the equipment. I laughed and pointed out I was not an officer and to stop calling me sir. We started the necessary repairs and worked until about two o'clock in the morning. While I had allowed him to take a few breaks that included meals, I had not eaten since the day before. So I asked if he knew where I was supposed to sleep. He answered yes, he was told where I was supposed to bunk. He took me to the officer's area and showed me a stateroom. As he left he reminded me that the officer galley was always open.

When I checked my room I found my bag was already in the room. So I made my way to the galley to make a sandwich. As I was in the fridge a chief petty officer came into the galley yelling about who was messing up his kitchen. I turned from the fridge and said, "Chief I was just looking for something to eat". When he saw me, he told me to go get a shower and he would bring me something to eat. When I got out of the shower I had a very nice meal in my room.

We finished all the repairs just before pulling into port. All that was left to do was test the equipment. While in port, testing is limited because steam demands cannot be changed enough to fully test the controls. The demands from the engine are required to allow for a correct test. So there was nothing for us to do until we pulled back out to sea where I could use the main engines to test the response of the controls.

Because of this limitation, while speaking with the chief engineer, I pointed out that I might like to have a couple of days of liberty while we were in port. I informed him that the repairs were made however testing couldn't be done until we returned to sea. I also pointed out that I had missed at least one payday and could use some cash as I didn't bring any. He said that was no problem and asked how much I wanted. I told him a couple hundred dollars would be wonderful and would work just fine. I received my pay advance and the second class I was working with and I went on liberty. Usually when in port we would only get one day of liberty, if we were lucky. So getting to spend three days on shore running around was great fun.

After the liberty, when we got back to the ship, we rechecked all our connections. The ship went out to sea which is when we got to test the controls. Testing the controls was the most fun of the project. You start with small incremental changes to the ship's engines like going from a stop to one third ahead. Back to stop. If everything works you try going from stop to two thirds. Then back to stop to make sure the boilers respond properly. By working correctly the boilers don't burn excessive amounts of fuel and stay within operating parameters. Too much pressure inside of a boiler can be hazardous to everyone working on it. It's also very hard on the physical attributes of the boiler. You slowly but surely increase your changes on the engines until you have reached the point that you're running from a full forward direction to a reverse direction. Moving a ship's engine like this is a pretty drastic maneuver. For some of the ships like a tin can (destroyer), especially when you go flank speed ahead to emergency stop is huge. An emergency stop is when all engines go from flank speed to full astern. Full astern was to take as much steam from the boilers as they can take.

After these tests were satisfactory completed, we turned ship's controls back over to the discretion of the captain and I was done on this particular ship. I thought no big deal, this was a nice long vacation, packed my bags, went and checked out with the engineering officer who took me to the Captain. I was taken to the flight deck and once again I hopped on a helicopter. Instead of returning to my ship, I went to another ship.

I spent the next seven months going from ship to ship throughout the Mediterranean Sea. When I started this I was timid and unsure of what my role was. I finished it with far more ego than I should have had the capacity to come up with. When we pulled into port and we had nothing to do, my request for funding grew drastically. I had lost all my opportunities for poker money by not being on my own ship. So I felt justified.

On the last ship I worked on before returning to my ship, we had completed all the repairs necessary for the system around two o'clock in the morning. I woke up around eight o'clock and went down to get my helper. I was informed that he was put back on the schedule and was up to ship's muster. To say that I was upset is an understatement. So here I am in my grubby little coveralls marching up to the flight deck to get my helper out of muster. He had suffered the heat and now I wanted him to do the fun stuff, which was testing everything.

I found the engineering officer, a Lieutenant Commander. He told me that our work was over so he had him returned to normal duty. This made me a little upset and I went on to degrade this Lieutenant Commander and remind him of the agreement the Captain and I had. The Captain was at muster and did nothing during my little tirade to this Lieutenant Commander.

So having recovered my helper, we went to the crew's quarters where

18

we changed and then went down to the boiler room. Testing went fine and there were no issues, so I returned the ship's controls to the captain. I packed up my bag, traveled to the flight deck and hopped on the helicopter. By this time I never knew where I was going when I hopped on a helicopter. This particular time, I returned to my home ship. This was two days before returning to the homeport of Little Creek, Virginia. I was just in time for a payday and mail call. Much to my surprise, I received seven months' worth of back pay and a large stockpile of mail that had arrived while I was off the ship. Upon arriving in port I was unlucky enough to secure first duty. First duty means that everybody else gets to go on leave and liberty and you have to get the engine room and boiler room secured, shut down and put into maintenance. Now ships generally rotate into two crews with the third crew allowed to take leave while the first two crews rotate duty days. I rotated out of the ship the next day.

After a couple of days of rotating duty crews, it's back to normal operations. I had a scheduled leave and was planning on flying to my home state. Normally I traveled in my dress uniform, mostly because that's the best I had with me. It is important to note that dress uniforms have our rank on them as well as your last name. As I was walking down the gangway to leave, a Lieutenant Commander was walking up the gangway. As we passed, protocol requires that I salute, which I did. The Lieutenant Commander returned the salute at which point he recognized me as the person that he took a tirade from. He then required me to return with him to the chief engineer's office.

It's important to note that the chief engineer is a Lieutenant which is a lesser rank than a Lieutenant Commander. The Lieutenant Commander was most upset that I, an enlisted man had humiliated him. He was very upset with being addressed in the manner in which I had spoken to him, especially with me being just an enlisted man. The Lieutenant Commander asked my chief engineer what he was going to do about it. The chief engineer leaned over and told me to go back to his ship undo everything I had done. I replied with a hearty "yes sir" and turned to leave. At that point Lieutenant Commander realizing that he would be in a big bind, let the matter drop and I was allowed to go on my leave.

4 THE END AND A NEW BEGINNING

When I returned from my leave, I was temporarily assigned to fleet maintenance group (FLEETMAG). Being the lowest ranking member on the totem pole, whenever there was a long sea call, I was assigned to go. This duty rotation lasted six months after which time, I was returned to my ship. Shortly after my arrival back on board ship, we were underway again.

During this particular cruise, we had many mechanical issues in the boiler room. Several pieces of equipment would break down at the same time causing the ship to have to reduce its speed. This also restricted the ship's maximum speed. As the flagship for the Sixth Fleet Atlantic, this was unacceptable. As one of the senior enlisted men on board ship, who knew this equipment, it was my responsibility to get the equipment up and running as quickly as possible. We tore apart one of the ships main boiler feed pumps, rebuilt it and got it back into service only to have another pump fail. While I was working on the second pump and into the second day of no sleep the assistant chief engineer handed me a couple of pink pills. He said they would keep me going. Every few hours, he would show up and hand me a couple of helpers and away I would go. As I recall I worked for well over 90 hours straight with my little helpers. At the end of this time, I had rebuilt all four of the boilers feedwater pumps and several other accessory pumps. It should be pointed out that when I say I did it, I mean as part of a team, I wasn't working alone. Several members of the team would rotate in and out of service to get some rest, have some downtime and then rotate back into the team. During this time, those on board who were unfamiliar with the equipment would be rotated through so that they could gain experience working on the pumps and turbines.

After so many hours of no rest and the medical aid I received from the assistant chief engineer, I could no longer function. As I was leaving the engine room to take a shower and go to get some sleep a Chief Warrant Officer decided to chastise me for my inability to make repairs. This chastising started as verbal and then became physical. When he thumped my chest I hit him. When he got up, I hit him again. He got up and I hit him again. A total of seven times I hit this Warrant Officer. Not very becoming actions I must say. I was then escorted to the chief engineer's office who started to verbally chastise me and he then thumped me in my chest, so I hit him. As I was hitting him, the Captain of the ship walked in. It should be noted that while all ships commanding officers are called Captain, this Captain was also a Captain in rank...a full bird Captain. He got my attention and was telling me how much trouble I was in. In my fatigue-induced state, I pulled back and was going to hit him. As I pulled back to strike the Captain, a friend of mine who had watched the whole shenanigan unfold, stopped my arm from going forward so I could not contact the Captain. It was clear that I tried. As you might expect I was thrown into the brig (aka jail). As they threw me in I thought, this place has air-conditioning, its own toilet room, a shower and I get three squares meals a day - I should've done this a week ago. After some time in the brig, I was awakened, given my dress uniform and told to prepare to go to Captain's mast. Captain mast is like a court-martial procedure.

As a side note when I was thrown into the brig, the automatic controls stopped working onboard our ship. So for the several days that I was in the brig getting cleaned up and recuperating for Captain's mast, the ship was running at a reduced speed. Even with the extra hours at which the engine room and boiler room were working, the ship was not running anywhere near top speed. Remember we were a flagship and the flagship carries the fleet's Admiral and staff officers. The entire Sixth Fleet was running with a reduced speed. Not good.

The executive officer was presiding over the Captain's mast because the Captain himself was involved in the charges. I was told I was not being kicked out of the Navy for assaulting a commissioned officer but that I was being given 30 days extra duty only to be seen served in port, 30 days of restriction (confined to ship), again, only to be served in port. And two-thirds of my pay was being removed for six months and a cut in rank from E5 to E1. E1 was less than the rank I had when I joined the Navy. The restriction would confine me to ship for an entire Mediterranean tour.

After Captain's mast, I was told I was no longer to be locked up, but ordered to go repair the ships automatic controls. I asked for this order in writing. Why would I ask for my orders in writing? They asked the same question. The reason I stated was "since I had disciplinary action, I no longer had security clearance. And the equipment I was being ordered to work on was classified. Also, without the proper security clearance, I could not have the designated job classification to work on this particular equipment. So before an undesignated, unsecured individual worked on classified equipment, they would need to have those orders in writing."

Absolutely not, was the response from the chief engineer and the executive officer. So I returned to my duties as a fireman. As an E1 (firemen recruit) I was back to beginning duties as a messenger in the boiler room. All a messenger could do was take readings on equipment and run and get whatever was necessary.

A couple of days later I was summoned to the Chief Engineer's office, I was told that only the Captain was still pressing charges and that my reduction in rank had been suspended. I was then ordered to make the necessary repairs. I again asked for the orders in writing. When asked why, I again explained that since I had disciplinary action, I no longer had security clearance. And the equipment I was being ordered to work on was classified. Also, without the proper security clearance, I could not have the designated job classification to work on this particular equipment. So before an undesignated, unsecured individual work on classified equipment, I'd like to have those orders in writing. I added that my father was a Marine and I was his only child that went into military service; he would be heartbroken if I did not get my good conduct medal.

During this time, the speed at which the entire fleet could travel had been reduced to the maximum speed of the Admiral's ship. That would be the ship I was on. The Admiral was getting upset that this ship's captain could not uphold the correct speed. During the entire time I was being disciplined, the crew, including myself, were working eight hours on duty four hours off. As you can imagine, that got tiring very fast.

During this same period, they had been trying to get someone from FLEETMAG to come to the ship and repair the controls. The Captain and Admiral had been trying to force them to send someone and were being told that no one was available. Also, since I was assigned to this ship, they should have me complete the repairs. When FLEETMAG was told that I was not doing the repairs because of the loss of my security clearance, FLEETMAG responded that it was not their problem. My dad's advice about being good at something was about to pay off.

A week or so had passed since my captain's mast, the Admiral could no longer allow the fleet to stay at this slower speed. Admiral transferred the Sixth Fleet Command Flag to another ship. The fleet moved back up to the faster speed and left us, my ship, behind. The next day I was called up to the Captain's office and told that this incident never happened. Now that this never happened I was ordered to make the necessary repairs. I thought it would be wise to see how this incident was "handled" in my personnel file.

When I asked to see my personnel file the Captain opened my file and ripped out six or seven pages. As I understand military documentation, this was a big no-no. After verifying there was indeed no mention of these incidents in my file, I returned to the boiler room and began checking the system. Watching my every move were more officers then I thought were stationed on the ship. Included was the Admiral, his staff, the captain, executive officer, chief engineer, and several others.

I was delighted having all of these officers watch as I climb around this hot boiler area. I mean, seriously, they had their working dress uniforms on, I don't know what they were thinking. Most of them knew the amount of time it would take to repair the control system. But there they were, all watching me do my thing.

After a few hours of climbing around and checking everything, you can imagine my surprise when I find nothing broken. I had hooked up my calibrated gauges to the final control panel, made one adjustment, threw a switch and turned the whole system back on.

To say they were upset is an understatement of epic proportions. So everything on the ship went back to normal for about a week. After a week or so I was summoned to the chief engineer's office, told to pack my bags, and I had been given orders to leave the ship. At this particular time, I was seriously thinking about making the Navy a career. I had started to look into Officer's Candidate School (OCS) and I discovered that if you quit a voluntary program during your current four years you were not allowed to enter an additional program during the next enlistment.

So I went back to my bunk area, got my seabag out, packed up all my stuff and said good-bye. Several asked where I was going and I said I didn't know, just that I had orders to leave the ship that day.

We agreed that it was not a big surprise that the Captain would do that after the embarrassment of having the Sixth Fleet Command Flag leave the ship.

When I got to the chief engineer's office and asked where I was going, he said that it was in my orders and I could look as I left. The only person that was not happy to see me leave, as far as officers were concerned, was the assistant chief engineer. He was the one that gave me the drugs to keep me awake to get the equipment repaired. He wished me the best and he also said he was sorry for my luck. So with a seabag in hand and orders under my arm, I walked off the ship.

Once off the ship, I opened my orders to see where I was supposed be going. Imagine my surprise when I read that I was to report to the SEALS base. First of all, in the early 1970s, nobody knew what the SEALs were, including me. At first, I thought it was a huge stroke of luck that I was going back in the Little Creek and would be fairly close to home. When I checked in at the commanding officers' area, I was welcomed aboard and thanked for volunteering. I told him I never volunteered for this and that I had no clue what this even was. At which time I was turned over to a chief petty officer and I told the chief the same thing. And then the fun began.

5 TRAINING

By fun, I mean the opposite of fun. The class I was assigned to was made up of about 125 men. All of these guys knew what they were getting into when they volunteered. Most had several months to prepare. They began physical fitness training long before they got there. I, on the other hand, had no idea of what we were about to go through. The weakest link on any team is the weakest person. At this point that was me.

We were placed into smaller groups called boat teams. These teams were put together with what appeared to be a total helter-skelter method. Some of the groups were similar in size and strengths, while others had the tallest paired with the shortest man. One group was made up of all men with the slightest build.

We were shown to our barracks, told to drop our gear and "fall out" in ten minutes. I saw some of the guys stripping out of dress uniforms into workout clothing. Then several of the others started to follow suit. I thought they might know more than me on what was about to happen. I also followed suit, while others from the class decided not to change. Their thought was: "If they wanted us to change they would have told us to change". It was a decision they would regret. We fell out for muster and we were introduced to the training POs (Petty Officers).

We started the first group activity with a five-mile run on the beach. Man, I was glad I changed. Several of the men asked to be allowed to change and were given the response that, "SEALs always adapt and adjust". Their request was denied and because they questioned the order, we now all dropped to the sand and gave 50 pushups. That was the beginning of several hours of physical training (PT).

I can't speak for the others but I'd be lying if I said I did 50 pushups. Then we were off on a five-mile run. If you've never run in the sand, it is a unique experience. It becomes even more unique when you have 75 or so guys in front you chewing up the sand. When we finished our run I would like to say we all felt really good about ourselves. But that would be a lie. I was in no condition to be doing this kind of physical training. Even the guys that knew they were going to be in this class and had a long time to prepare were struggling. So you can just imagine how the rest of us were. I never knew that too much exercise can make you vomit. Just goes to show, you learn something new every day.

At the end of a run, they told us we could cool down and go for a "swim." We soon learned that "go for a swim" did not mean a relaxing time in the ocean. They meant immediately jump in the cold ocean. It is important to remember these oceans have surf. Surf is different than just waves. Waves are caused by wind, surf is caused by wind and tides. Surf near the shoreline can get rough. We would lay in the surf - later we were taught to lock arms with our buddies for control -but not this time. The guys still in their uniforms were carrying around a lot of extra weight from the wet wool. I was getting sand in all the wrong places. We were ordered to come out of the surf and roll in the sand. After rolling awhile, we would do some form of exercise then back into the surf. We did this for what seemed like hours. After a while, we were told that we could go to the barracks and get ready for chow.

So like the idiots we were at this point, we did as we were told and we started moving towards the barracks. After all, we knew where they were. We were then asked what the hell we were doing and told that while we were there, we were to go nowhere without carrying our telephone pole. Each boat team group was then assigned a telephone pole. You were to pick it up above your head and take it with you wherever you went.

Oh yeah, I almost forgot to mention you never walk anyplace. You ran. We had started to the barracks without our telephone pole (it should be pointed out the pole had a slang term for a unique member of the male anatomy). Because we decided to leave without carrying our pole, and we were walking, that cost us another 50 push-ups. Someone argued that we did not know we had to carry a pole when we originally told to head to the barracks. We dropped and did yet another 50 push-ups.

We got to the barracks and those of us that could change into dry clothes did. The guys that were still in their dress uniforms did their best to salvage their dress uniforms and change into working uniforms. Several of the guys made it into the head to throw up. Not all but many. At which point we were called out for muster again. By the way, not even ten minutes had passed.

It was at this muster that the rules of the camp were explained to us. Any man could quit, stop training and walk away. All that man had to do was ring a big ships style bell. The bell was found in prominent view of our training area. Once the bell was rung it could not be un-rung. Meaning you could not change your mind. Once the bell was rung you were no longer assigned to this unit and you would be given new orders to return to your primary job within a few days. In addition, you would not be allowed to stay in the area or return to the area.

I raised my concern, again, that I had never volunteered for this assignment, therefore, I should not be held to those standards. How could I possibly quit an all-volunteer group that I didn't volunteer for? Let me just add as a sidebar that when you're in a unit like this making yourself an obvious target to the instructors and trainers is a bad idea. No - a seriously terrible idea.

Another 50 push-ups. Not just for me but my entire class. I probably should have read the book on how to make friends and influence people before I started this endeavor.

All the fitness training we did was as a large group. We worked with our group and the groups worked with the class. The groups did everything together as a class. The first few weeks all we did was run, swim, roll in wet sand, pushups, pull-ups, planks, and leg lifts. They were grueling days and nights of physical conditioning. Every day I would check to see if I had new orders. Every day I was told the same thing. No, but I could ring the bell and quit. It seemed that getting someone to ring out was a point of pride to these POs. During this phase of the training, I cannot recall the number of guys that "rang out". The class size was around half after the first few weeks. I would start every day thinking I only have to make it through the day because my orders will be here tonight. If I quit I could not go to college and become an officer.

This is also when we started our water training and I was glad about it. I was a high school swimming team member, lifeguard, swimming instructor, and I grew up on a lake. I also had played around with SCUBA gear since I was fourteen. The water and I were buddies, or so I thought. It was not long before they took that idea away from me with this training.

Our first exposure to the pool was to tread water. Treading water doesn't sound bad. But these guys like to add an evil twist to EVERYTHING. Try treading water holding your arms over your head. Okay, that's not too bad. Try it for a 15-minute-long session. During the 15 minutes if anyone's elbows touch the water the clock would reset. Oh did I mention you don't get a rest between clock resets?

After several sessions, you get good with your elbows out and you feel good about yourself. Then we had to do it with a five-pound block. Again after a few sessions, you're doing okay with a five-pound block. Then let's move the block to ten pounds. Oh yeah, I forgot to tell you, the time increased as well.

We lost men all the time now. We would be near finishing a training or exercise session and somebody would be at the bell. Usually, those of us that were closest would try to encourage them not to quit. I don't ever remember someone that started walking to the bell stop and return to the team.

So now each day started with our normal, brisk, five-mile run and or an open ocean swim before breakfast. Breakfast was followed by an hour or three of physical training. One day without warning they changed things up on us. That morning we were broken into new small groups. Our old telephone pole group was separated. Once we were divided into these new small groups. We were separated into smaller groups and began more specialized training.

Now every day began one of two ways. We would wake up, or more accurately - we would get forced up; light calisthenics to loosen up, and then off to the beach for a morning run before breakfast or instead of a run, we would do an open ocean swim. After that we would be off to chow. After chow, it would be more training that varied from day-to-day. It might be weapons training, hand-to-hand training, or classroom work to learn various academic skills.

Early on in the hand-to-hand training, we were trained in knife fighting. One day as we were sitting around watching the instructors give us the fundamentals of a knife fight, I remember thinking that at least this is something I've done before. Then the instructors said, "get up here and let's see what you got". They were pointing at me. I was shocked. I remembered the two things my father always told me about going into the military. Number one - don't volunteer for anything. If that didn't work well find something to be the best at. Even if it's cleaning a toilet.

So here I was, on the training platform. The instructor threw me a fairly large knife. It was a plastic-type knife with the blade that collapsed into the handle. When the blade collapsed into the handle it was supposed to leave an ink mark. The wider the ink mark, the deeper the cut would have been. Purple was the color of the ink that this particular knife was loaded with.

I learned to knife fight on the street and do not have a conventional style of holding a knife. My stance was also unconventional. I was not "refined" in knife fighting technique. So when I was given the knife and told to fight, the POs ridiculed me for my stance and method of holding the knife. I was being mocked and being told that this was much different from what the military taught. I tried to explain that in the street, killing was not the primary objective, survival was. Wounding, maiming, or serious injury was the objective. That's a fundamental difference between civilian versus military style that I was learning. The real lesson here for me was don't talk back to instructors. Lesson two: Don't piss off your instructors.

One thing that had always worked in my favor was my speed. I am a fairly big boy. I was six feet six inches tall and weighed around two hundred and twenty-five pounds. I learned that most people my size have much slower reflexes than I do. The training instructor, however, took my unorthodox stance as being inept with a knife. So when he challenged my position, I countered his swing and took a small cut to my hand. But, I was able to place a two-inch-wide purple band around his neck. In the real world, this would've been good. Good, because I would have quickly killed my opponent. In a training environment, where I was going to be with the same training instructor for an extensive period of time, this was a bad idea, no, not a bad idea, a terrible idea.

From that point on, whenever the instructor needed someone to demonstrate, I was the guinea pig. As a guinea pig, I was given no chance to defend myself. Looking back, it is surprising I survived being the training example.

Here's one scenario; we were learning a hand to hand technique. We were sparing with three-foot poles that were padded on the ends. They looked like large q-tips. The instructor called my name. As I'm walking up to the training area, I was handed a q-tip while getting hit by the instructor. The instructor would then add something like, "you always have to be on guard".

Hindsight, that added training/butt whipping served me well. At the time, all I could hear is my father telling me to not volunteer. It took a while, but, I was finally understanding what he meant. "Don't be the first" and now I was messing that up. Still, every day I would tell myself the same thing. I only need to make it through today. My orders will probably be here tonight. If I quit I cannot become an officer, I cannot make the Navy a career. For me, that was a very motivating force.

The only time this philosophy was seriously tested was during what's now known as hell week. The advantage during hell week is that you're so busy and so tired you don't think about anything else except putting one foot in front of the other. In the process of writing this book, I've been trying to remember how many guys we lost during hell week. I honestly don't have a clue. Between being so busy and so tired, the crews changed drastically during that period of time. You lose track of people that aren't immediately in front of you. At least I did.

After hell week I would like to say, things settle down a little bit. But that would not even be close to the truth. One thing I did notice after this week was that we were not losing people from our class every day. We were a much smaller group. To me, that's when we started to gel as a group and a unit. The training got much more intense, much more involved, and far more detailed. The little detail points that were not highlighted earlier were now required to be dealt with. Everything was fine-tuned from that point forward.

It's like making a knife sharp. You use a lot of really big broad strokes to get the knife the shape that you want. After you have the shape, you start honing the edge to be razor-sharp. That's what I felt the last part of our training was all about - making us razor-sharp. I've heard people talk about "getting at the edge" or "you must hold the edge". That was the edge they were trying to get us to: to the edge of being razor-sharp. It's the edge that made it possible for us to do what we did.

Even during hell week, every day, I had the same question. Did my orders come? No. Ok, tomorrow then. I only have to make it through today. After the completion of hell week, my attitude started to change a little bit. I still asked the question every day. I still thought I only had to make it through the day because I'd have my new orders by that night. But the grueling day-to-day had become a lot less difficult. Oh, don't get me wrong it was not easy, just less difficult. I honestly believe if I didn't have the attitude that I only have to do this until tomorrow I would have never made it through. I would've quit.

After hell week it was becoming almost fun. The keyword there is almost. With about six or eight weeks left in basic, I was called to the commanding officer's office. The orders that I had been waiting for all this time had come. The commanding officer asked, "Did you know you never volunteered?" Really, he asked me that question. What did he think I was talking about for the last five months? But, because I was one of the few that had completed this much of the training, I was asked, "How would you like to volunteer for SEALs training?" I did not have to think long or hard. "Absolutely" was my response. I know it goes against the grain. I mean I have been trying for five months to get out of this stupid program. Now, to stay in it without an issue, well, it seemed like a good idea at the time.

So there I was a brand-new SEAL, just completed basic. I was taken out of basic training and placed into the teams. I was assigned to team 2. This suited me just fine as it was in Little Creek and that's where my home was. Now, I could get off the base. Now, I could tell people what I was doing. Well a little bit. Oh what fun it was to show up to the clubhouse in your brand-new work uniforms with your brand-new trident on your shirt having gone through all this training thinking you're really somebody. Thinking that while this was not what I originally wanted, I am a member of the club now! To be met, with mild amusement, by guys who are hardened warriors. While they respect what I had completed, they didn't respect me.

I got off the base and headed for home only to find that my wife has moved in with her boyfriend. One reason I wanted to go to college and become an officer was to make a better life for my family. When

I left the apartment several months ago, I was headed to the Mediterranean Sea for a for a six month cruise and then I was to go home. After the six months of training I arrived at my apartment to find that my wife was gone, family plans destroyed, not quite what I was expecting. So I did what most people do in such a situation. I got drunk.

At this time in my life I could consume large quantities of adult beverages with little to no affect. I can remember only three times in my life that I was drunk. One was while I was still in high school, this time, and the last time was much later in life. This time, I woke up the next morning half naked, on the beach.

6 FIRST MISSION

So one day you are out of basic and graduated as a "real SEAL" thinking you're all big and bad. Then you meet the guys who are all that and more and you see how inadequate you really are. And why you don't want to think about it. These guys are the real bad asses. They've seen combat. They have seen missions, been out there in the real world doing real things. One thing you learn early on is that people who have seen and done the stuff, the real life stuff that SEALs have to do, hate it and don't talk about it. Especially with people that have not been there. I remember thinking yeah that's what I want to be when I grow up.

While I won't say they were downright hostile to me when I came in, they were not the friendliest folks either. Looking back I can understand why. But at the time I thought we are all members of the same club. While we were all members of the same club, we weren't all at the same level within that club. That would come later. Maybe…if you earned it.

So one day we got to called to gear up. We had some equipment to recover. So we showed up where we were told to be. Our gear ready to go. We took a helicopter out into the bay to a crash site. This was a simple recovery. We were to pick up ordnance and the pilot's remains. So we jumped in the water. I was in the water probably 30 minutes looking for anything to recover. Then I spot a helmet. Being the green new guy that I was and having no idea what I am doing. I swam over, picked up the helmet took it back to the basket and placed it in. When what to my wondering eyes should I see? We see the pilots head rolling out of the helmet.

I remember thinking, just a few days ago I thought I was a Mister Somebody. A real bad ass. Well this Mr. Somebody ended up underwater tossing his cookies. So here I was on my first mission on scuba gear, tossing my cookies. Holding the regulators in my mouth. Puking. Not a fun little process. Nope it's not the least bit of fun at all. After I regain my composure, the rest of the recovery goes without a hitch. We recovered all the tactical gear we were supposed to and the rest of the pilot's remains, got picked up by the helicopter and returned to base.

A few days later I was told that I'm part of a group that's going back to the Mediterranean Sea. Our mission is to check and test base and ship security. I'm specifically told to take my old working blue uniforms with all of my old rankings on it.

Our arrival was timed so we would be able to test the security at the changing of command of sixth fleet. When a changing of command takes place, a lot of officers are in the same place at the same time. You have the incoming sixth fleet admiral and his staff, the outgoing admiral, his staff, and also the officers from the area commands and affected ships.

Our rules of engagement we're explained to us on the flight over. They were indeed quite simple. Test the security of whatever it is were going up against. It could be a ship, it could be a base, it could be several ships. It didn't matter. Gaining access without an escort or losing the escort was our goal. We were to infiltrate and do damage. We had to have altered documents. Specifically our ID cards were not to be normal US issued. They had to have some flaw. The only other rules we had, was we either had to bring with us or steal from the ship whatever we needed to disable it and remove as much of the command structure as possible.

While most members of the team were well seasoned, others like me were not. You can imagine my surprise and my delight to find out the first test was on my old ship, the one whose Captain sent me to SEALs basic training as a punishment.

We were working in small two or three-man teams. Once onboard we were to either lose our escorts or get on without one. The rules for the ship were quite easy. No visitors were left un-escorted.

When an intruder is found or discovered, the quarterdeck is notified of the intruder. The quarterdeck then sounds the alert. All shipboard personnel are to stand fast. Stand fast means stay where you are on the ship and be prepared to present identification that you are on the ship that you are supposed to be on.

Walking up the gangway I was pleased to see that I knew the officer of the deck. After some initial formalities we told him that we were headed to the boiler room to work on the automatic combustion controls. We were then allowed to leave the quarterdeck unescorted.

This means that we had the run of the ship. This is a huge break in protocol. The plan of attack, since we had no equipment with us, was to steal what we wanted from the ships. This involved us getting to the armory and taking what we wanted. Taking meant we used masking tape to cover everything we would have taken. We then went to the engine rooms and several other key areas of the ship and planted makeshift explosive devices.

Our goal was never to sink the ship but to disable it. So we placed mock explosives in several key areas of the ship. We then went to officer's country to see what havoc we could raise on the command structure. Twice on our way to officer's mess room we were confronted by security personnel. Both times we simply identified we had information for the Captain on the ships automatic combustion controls. We were allowed to pass.

Outside the officer's mess were two armed Marine guards. We pointed our pretend guns at them and said "bang bang" you're both dead. We showed them copies of our orders and told them to sit down. Being good Marines they sat down. We then opened the door to the officer's mess, tossed in our paper hand grenades pointed our fingers and again said, "bang bang bang bang" you're all dead. I then had the delight of asking to see the Captain of the ship and I presented him his copies of the orders that stated that this was a training exercise. On presenting the Captain our orders, we identified ourselves as part of the SEAL team there to test the ship security plan. We also told him that we had planted several explosive devices throughout the ship.

In the officer's mess were both oncoming and off-going admirals of the sixth fleet, their supporting officer staff, the Captain's of each vessel both ongoing and incoming, several local command officers as well as my immediate commanding officer. My current commanding officer he had huge smile. He was the only one that had a smile.

For the next several months we moved around the Mediterranean Sea testing the security of naval bases and ships in port. I was amazed how easy it was for me to gain access to ships and bases. Maybe it was because I was easily identified as an American or we were not at war. Whatever the reason I developed a knack for convincing people that I belonged where I wasn't supposed to be.

Also during this period of time I got my handle or nickname. We were sent out into the bush for a few weeks of survival observation training. Ok, it wasn't really the bush, it was much more the mountains. But that is what we called it.

We had to survive on what we had or what we could find. Contacting any of the locals equaled mission failure. Being reported by the locals equaled mission failure. This was a live off the land exercise.

We had several targets that we were to keep track of. Recon as it is sometimes called. Anything we were going to eat had to be gotten without using our firearms. The sounds that they make when fired would have been a giveaway that we were in the area. And that would equal mission failed.

It was after several weeks of playing in the dirt we were told to report to our extraction point. We landed on a ship just as they were having breakfast. Looking back now we must have been a sight. I mean here we are straight out of the field, fully loaded for combat, haven't showered in weeks. Remember that in the 1970s SEALs were an unknown commodity. Thinking about how we looked and acted still makes me laugh.

Anyway we got in the chow line. In case you didn't know, enlisted personnel eat. They eat cafeteria style. So we got in line and were going to wait our turn when we were told to go ahead of everybody else. Funny thing was, nobody objected. Breakfast was traditional eggs, bacon, potatoes, and toast.

I got my chow and sat at the table with the rest of the team, when a 1st class petty officer stops at our table and starts to tell us how uncivilized we were. I mean, imagine the sight. This spit and polished sailor standing in front of us with his tray in his hands calling us filthy animals. So I reached up with my dirty hand, grab his over easy eggs and pushed them into my mouth.

Ok, truth be told I put most of them on my face and beard. The look on his face was priceless. He called me an animal and left. My teammates said he was right. And from that point on that's what I was called. Animal.

7 SKIING, GITMO, & A RAT

Looking back on my life during this period has been interesting to me. After the Med, I was back to Little Creek for a while. Days were busy with workouts, weapons training, bookwork, hand-to-hand training, and water training. Training was our life – it's what we did. The day would start with a swim or run or sometimes both. Then there was hand and mind work of some kind. It could have been weapons, timers, language, maps skills, jump training. It varied but you get the idea. Some days would not be days at all. We would go play at night.

I remember times we were in the clubhouse and some officers would come in. Usually when officers showed up it meant something was about to happen. Sometimes good, sometimes not so good. Sometimes they got us together and asked us questions. One time they asked if anyone skied. I remembered my dad telling me not to volunteer. But I remembered too late. Before I knew it I said, "I've skied". In all, I think a handful of us said we had skied. Which lead to the next question "Was it snow skiing?"

I had been snow skiing as an adolescent, so of course, I said yes. At which point we were told to gear up for cold weather and fall out in thirty minutes. When the gear up order is given most of the time you did not know what you were gearing up for. So, you grabbed anything that might be helpful. You could always (well almost always) leave what you did not need after the briefing. For this gear up, they had asked about snow skiing so I was thinking cold. I did not have much cold-weather gear lying around Little Creek, Virginia. But I'd learned to get by as best I could.

Then on to transport for another trip overseas. People that think travel is fun should ride in military transport planes. All the comforts of the woods. After we landed in Switzerland (I think) we got chow and a couple of lessons on our new skies. I don't know about other branches but navy transports lack for comfort a lot. We received a ski lesson. How to put on skies, start, stop, and how to fall. That's about it. After all, we already said we were skiers right?

After lunch, we geared up and headed to the helicopter for a ride up the mountain to go skiing. I remember thinking this had "bad idea" written all over it. We flew about halfway up the mountain and the helicopter hovered. We roped up, repelled out and were to ski down. This was almost beginning to be fun. Skies on our backs, snow boots on our feet and we were repelling down. What could possibly go wrong? The snow was clean and track free when we hit it. The snow was a lot deeper than I thought and not as hard-packed as I was used to. Let's just say working up a sweat in the cold mountain is not a good idea.

When we figured out how to get our skies on and off, we went. The skiing was physically hard because of the depth of the snow. The upside was we were not going very fast. I was glad I did not lead. It was pretty much a low slope area of the mountain. When we got back to camp we were told to gear down, grab some chow and get some rest.

We made another run the next morning. This time we tried jumping from the helicopter with our skis on; better idea but not without its problems. This run went awhile once we got moving. Back at camp, we were told to get ready for another run, this time in full combat gear. This extra 100 pounds or so changed everything, but we made it back to camp. When we got back to camp we were again told to gear down, grab some chow and get some rest.

We were told to get some sleep because we were going night skiing. Night skiing how bad could it be? Oh silly, silly sailor. Our first runs were fairly easy. We made a couple of runs and night skiing gave way to the day and everything seemed to be going ok. Then it was back to base and the chow hall.

I think officers sat around having a cigar in one hand and a drink in the other and someone asks, "Do you think that we could put people into a mission by having them ski with full combat gear?" So there we were, seated in the helicopter, ready for war, wondering why but still doing as we are told.

We skied down the mountain and everything was wonderful. Said not one of us. As I recall, only two of us skied to the extraction point. The others were picked up as they were checked in and gave them their location and their status. Most were out of the training operation because of equipment failure as opposed to injuries. At the time I did not think recreational skis were designed for this kind of impact. As an example, I broke my binding on the last drop to the extraction point. I slid and bounced the final yards. This was not a good position to be in if indeed we were going into combat. With our ski vacation over, we returned to Little Creek. We were not at the Creek long when some of us received the gear up order. It seems we were off to Guantanamo Bay, Cuba.

I have been trying to recall why we were sent to Guantanamo Bay Naval Station in Cuba. As hard as I try, I cannot recall why we were sent to that station. It had to be to complete some training or to conduct some training, I honestly cannot remember. These holes in my memory are one reason for this book. However, not being able to recall does seem to bother me less and less.

Anyway, we were in Guantanamo Bay or Gitmo. Whatever the reason was, we seemed to have a lot of free time. The base did have almost all the comforts of home. There were stores that you would find at any base, a place to eat, a couple of places to drink, a limited assortment of adult beverages, and a nice beach.

Gitmo is surrounded on roughly three sides with fences. The fences are protected by a guard tower staffed 24/7 by Marines. On the other side of the fences, the Cubans have similar towers. In addition to our towers, we also have the fence patrolled by roving marines. On the Cuba side of the fence, near the water was an active minefield. One day a few of us were talking and the idea of playing with the Cubans came up.

"Let's dig up the mines and move them", someone said. We can flip the warning sign around and hide the mine in a different place. Great idea, right? What could possibly go wrong?

We set up a night dive and dove out past the end of the fences. We came up to the beach, located and removed the Cuban mines. We flipped the sign, hid the mines and dove back around the fences. All without getting caught.

The next morning when the Cubans made their rounds they found someone had been in the minefield (our idea of fun). We sat on our beach and watched the show as they tried to locate and repair our little bit of fun. I know, sick, but we were who we were.

A couple of days later we thought, "let's do that again". So we set up a night dive. Dove out past the end of the fences. Came up to the beach. Located and removed the Cuban mines. Flipped the sign around, hid the mines and dove back around the fences. All without getting caught. Again.

The next morning we were all set to watch the show when our presence was requested in the Executive Officer's office. We were asked what we had to do with any of the issues the Cubans were upset about. We asked, "What are they upset about?" We were told how being outside the base was not legal and removing their military hardware is stupid and foolish.

Of course, as we were the most "let's play nice together groups" in the military, we reiterated that we knew nothing about it. We were reminded that entering onto the island of Cuba was not only unlawful it could heighten a conflict. As we agreed, we also confessed it was not us. Now that we had been officially chastised, warned and not caught, you can bet we were going to do it again. So we waited a few days before going on a night dive again. This time we thought we might rev things up a bit. So some of us brought their quiet rifles. A quiet rifle is one with a silencer fitted onto it. We set up a night dive. Dove out past the end of the fences. Come up to the beach. Removed the Cuban mines. Flipped the sign around. But instead of returning to the water we snuck under the Cuban's guard tower and shot out a couple of the United States side guard lights.

This caused the US Marines to get pissed and of course, they replied in kind. The reply was shooting out some of the Cuban's lights. Neither the Marines nor the Cuban's had quiet rifles so things got loud fast. The Cubans had no idea why the Marines did this, so they responded by doing the same. I can only guess that some officers started giving orders, probably on both sides and things went back to normal.

We made our way back to the beach relocated the mines, got into the water and dove out around the fence. As we were coming out of the water we were met with a party. Naval shore patrol and a group from the marines. They questioned us about what we were doing and we answered "training".

As we were escorted back to our barracks. I remember thinking maybe we went a little too far this time. However as morning came, no one was at the door so we set off on our run. Shortly after we started, however, our run was stopped short. We were given orders to return to Little Creek. I guess that meant our fun in Gitmo was over.

We were at the clubhouse in Little Creek when we were told to gear up. We were going to be temporary guards on a ship that was going into the shipyard. We were only to be on it for a few days while they arranged to offload some weapons. The ship's crew had already gone somewhere. The Marines that were assigned to this ship were going to be relieved by us.

We guessed the duties would be pretty simple. I mean we were in a secured naval shipyard so no problem right? We arrived and relieved the marines. A guard plan was made and we got to work.

If you have never been in a shipyard like this; I will try to describe it. The ships sit on a long pier (like a really big dock). The pier is long enough for more than one ship on each side. The yard has several piers and a couple of dry-docks. A dry-dock is like a smaller pier that comes out of the water.

Most ships still have people living on them. Some are just coming in and others are getting ready to leave. The pier allows trucks to deliver supplies and remove trash. The pier also allows for large equipment to be loaded or unloaded. A lot is going on, on at the pier during the day. At night, not so much.

As trash is offloaded it is stacked in large piles, in several locations along the pier. Many times, a sailor with too much to drink has passed out in these piles. Like I said, we were assigned as guards for this ship. My assignment was the quarterdeck from 12 o'clock until 4 o'clock. Yep, that's twice a day.

So I was on duty during the 0000 till 0400 watch, when I saw what looked like a small dog. I think to myself, "What is a dog doing in the shipyard?" As the animal moves down the pier a little closer to me, I see that it's not a dog, it's a big cat. As it moves to the next pile I see that it's a rat. I remember thinking guys pass out in these trash piles, this rat could kill them. So I pulled out my weapon, took aim and fired.

The rat went flying. To my surprise, it turned, bared its teeth and started walking towards me. So I fired again. I knew I made contact because it went flying again. But the damn thing turned and stared back at me. I knew from that first clip I hit it at least ten times. As I was putting the next clip in, I felt a hand on my shoulder.

It was my entire team. They heard the shots and came running to repel all of the boarders. When I lowered my weapon I was asked why I killed the dog. I replied that it was a rat. One of my teammates went and picked up the rat and was going to show it to me. I told him that I would shoot him first.

When base security arrived, we had everything back to normal. We asked them what all the shooting was about. I am pretty sure they knew it was us. I don't think they believed that it was not us. But that's our story and we stuck by it.

8 TAG & SUB

People would ask me if I have ever been to "such and such" country. I used to answer with, "I don't know". That would get me a look of attitude. I think that people thought I was keeping a secret. The truth was I really didn't know.

We were often loaded on to a plane with no windows and flown to where we would be "training". Or we would board a ship or submarine to do what we had to do. After the "training" we would return to an assigned point. This was often done with little to no contact with locals. The military personnel we met were as task-focused as we were and the actual country we were in had no bearing. At least that was my attitude.

Also when we traveled we kept to ourselves. I think we were seen as having an elitist attitude. While it is true that SEALs are a highly trained elite group, most of my memories were not that we thought we were better than anybody - only different. Also, we were kept apart from other military personnel for other reasons. Security was one reason. Another was we did not look, dress or act like regular Navy personnel.

One time we were attached to the fleet for a training exercise to practice placing magnetic devices onto the bottom of other ships. We were at a joint NATO training exercise. During this exercise, the Warsaw Pact was conducting a training exercise in the same area.

Our training was to see if we could deliver a device that could be easily attached to a ship's hull. The device would have one of two effects. It would either mimic an explosive device or interrupt sonar.

In addition to the attachment, we were to determine how long it took for a response to be started and what that response was. There is some inherent risk in doing an exercise like this. Ships use seawater for several things like supplying the boilers with cooling water. And the boilers supply power to the ship.

This seawater gets pulled into the ships by way of large intakes that are attached to large pumps which suck the water into the ship. There are usually several of the intakes under a ship. Also, the ship's screws or propellers can move at any time.

Getting pulled into an intake would be a bad thing. It would be game over for the game or mission. It would also be a huge embarrassment for the individual. Not to mention the physical damage that could happen to the diver. You would at least be cut up pretty bad. Worst case, you could be killed.

So we had to get into the water, dive down and over to the correct ship, attach a magnetic (fake) bomb, not get sucked in and return to the correct ship, all the while, not being seen or getting caught. It is important to remember that all of our ships had the same hazards when you swam under them.

Divers entering the water is not something that people see a lot, so it can create quite a stir even in the Navy. An added challenge was finding a valid reason for being seen entering the water. Because we were on a Landing Platform Dock (LPD) we could use the motor well to leave and return to. But to do so would require the dock to be used for another reason. So as the marines did landing training we would play our game.

We were given the gear up command and we set off to play our game. We had been given our targets based on what would cause the most disruption for the "enemy" fleet. In between landing craft operations, we went for a swim. The operation went off without a hitch. It was very comical how the tagged ship reacted. The majority of our people had no idea of what these ships were doing. The common comment I heard was they were doing some kind of training exercise. I guess in a way they were.

Another aspect of the training operation was to talk to other sailors from the Warsaw pack. During the 1970s most US Navy personnel were discouraged from socializing with the "enemy". It was part of our training exercise to gather any information that we could.

The information we collected was not the stuff from James Bond movies, but rather where people were from, how long had they been in the Navy, what training did they have. Stuff like that.

It was humorous to me that the sailors we were talking to were most likely our counterparts, doing the same thing we were doing. We sat around and had a few beers and talked about our Navies trying to get them to say something of use, all the while making sure we didn't say something we shouldn't.

9 CYPRUS

One day while we were in Little Creek the call came in to gear up. Our team was going on a joint training session with NATO. While we were playing around with the NATO games, we were given a briefing about a possible evacuation mission on the island of Cyprus. The United States Embassy was in danger of being overrun. We were to prepare for an evacuation of the compound. We were told we would be the closest team to the island and to be geared up and ready. The NATO games had concluded and we were on standby.

The ship we had been assigned to was going to remain our home for the next few days. As we pulled out of the NATO games, the ship was scheduled to be resupplied at sea. However, while we were in route to the resupply location, the ship was diverted to Cyprus, which meant no new food for us.

We made our mission plan based on the information we had from the military intelligence community. This was my first direct contact with these military intelligence folks. After we had completed the mission I had a better understanding of the running jokes associated with these idiots. But more on them later.

We geared up and headed to the boats and waited twelve to fifteen hours. Then came the stand-down order. Only a few people realize that when you get geared up, the body goes through a process. Some of the steps most people understand, others not so much. You load up with water, food, ammunition and other supplies that you need. You also learn to use the toilet facilities and making sure your bladder and GI tract are as empty as possible. I am explaining this so you understand that when you gear up, it is not just a matter of grabbing your gun and leaving. It really is a process. So we stood down. We were told that the ship was headed for resupply. We broke down and stored all of our gear.

I don't know how it is today, but in those days, very few people knew what a SEAL was. We were fairly isolated from the rest of the ship's personnel. On our way to be resupplied, we were again diverted back to Cyprus. It's funny to me that by now all of the fresh food supplies had been depleted. The entire ship (ok the enlisted) were eating rice and roast beef. I know what you are thinking - rice and roast beef sounds pretty good. I agree except we went through this entire gear up, stand down process. Heading for resupply took 24 days. The ship served rice and roast beef for breakfast. Rice and roast beef for lunch. Rice and roast beef for supper. We had rice and roast beef every possible way you can think of.

In addition to the monotony of rice and roast beef, don't forget the repeated briefings, the changing deployment plans, and the gear up gear down scenarios. The gear up process was more than just preparing equipment. It was a mental and physical preparation as well. It almost became routine to gear up just to gear down. A couple of times we even made it into the boats to launch. We planned for a beach landing. We planned for a dock landing. We planned for a swimming landing. We planned for-- I think you get the idea. We planned. And still just waited. Not much in my life was more frustrating than getting ready to do the job I trained for and being told "maybe tomorrow". It was like I was back in SEALs basic only in reverse.

Military intelligence kept us informed of the ongoing changes on the island, updating us to the changing mission parameters and what we could expect as we landed on the island. One evening, or morning, we were told to head to a briefing again. We were to plan for a landing at the existing pier. At this briefing, we were informed that no officers would be on this landing. The lack of officers was not unusual for us but the fact that we were being informed about the lack of officers was. The lack of officers was for deniability if things went wrong. That was new. The plan was to take the launches (similar to WWII landing craft) straight up to the dock. Demonstrate that we had and were firing live ammunition. This is where the orders got a little different. We were to make our way to the Embassy, using whatever force we felt necessary.

We were given the plan and the green light to go. I got to pick which gun mount I wanted, I chose the front mount. I chose the front gun mount because the front mount would fire into the trees, then the craft would turn and tie up at the dock. The landing craft would turn so it could tie off to the pier for a quicker return to the ships. Also as we turned to dock I would be unable to fire. The other mounts would be responsible for setting the tone if the conflict escalated. In case you don't remember - I got into the teams by listening to an officer who had a plan.

Again military intelligence was at the top of their game. No pier. So the plans changed just that quickly. There is a term for that in the military. It is fubar. That's what happened on this part of the mission.

As we approached the shore, just off the beach stood a small group of trees. Between the trees and the beach, there was a large number of rebels. We picked a height of about fifteen feet, turned two, twin mounted, 50 caliber machine guns and shot into the trees. The resulting response from the beach was surprising. The beach emptied.

After we landed we made our way to the Embassy unopposed. We reinforced the Embassy detachment, notified fleet command and waited. Shortly after we set up a perimeter. Marines from the fleet landed and set up an evacuation route.

As the Embassy staff did their thing, getting the placed closed up, we relieved the Embassy security staff to allow them to recover. Our assignment was to maintain the security of the Embassy. Others had begun evacuating those in the Embassy to the ships that were waiting offshore.

Once everyone was loaded on the ships we were cleared to leave as well. I was one of the first to arrive back onboard the ship. As I was packing up my gear one of the teammates said that we left an American on the beach. I thought he was joking, turned out he wasn't. It seems a young Marine lieutenant saw that his passport was expired and denied him permission to board.

Keep in mind we evacuated everyone from the island that wanted to go; Americans and nationals and others. To say we were pissed is a gross understatement. We had been planning on this mission for days and then to leave an American behind was unacceptable. This lieutenant needed to go for a swim. Several from the team went looking this a-hole. We approached command with the question of whether this was true. We were informed that it was indeed true. They (command) were working on a fix. So here we are steaming away from an American that is alone and unarmed.

What's a SEAL to do? We geared up. Because I had been stationed on similar ships I had a plan. Also, me and rules were not such good friends. We launched a landing craft without permission and were underway. As we approached the beach we could see our American friend all alone and the rebel's starting to move in. So we opened up again with the '50s.

If you have never seen what a large quantity of 50 caliber rounds can do - it can make trimming trees fun. Again the rebels left. Our new best friend dove to the sand for cover. After we picked him up we headed back to the ship and our troubles. As we moved out to sea the rebels began returning fire. Part of me wanted to play the game and show them what we were all about. But as we were well out of their range cooler minds prevailed.

When we arrived back at the waiting ship and as I pulled into the ships launching well; we were greeted by armed marines. Also present was our command structure. As we escorted our American friend he was telling all that would listen that we had saved his life. Not really a true statement but he felt it was.

Also greeting our return was the rest of the team who were also armed. Joining the party were several marine guards, they too were armed. Can you say awkward? After some brief name-calling and what turned out to be idle threats, we went to stow our gear. While en route, the question came up about the lieutenant that caused the problem in the first place. Did he get found and did he go for a swim. Loosely put, going for a swim means throwing him overboard. It turns out we were not the only ones looking for him. They (command) found him first. Shortly after we left for our unauthorized boat ride he was flown to another ship, never to be heard from again. No action was taken against us and we left the ship a few days later.

10 TURKEY

My next, and what would be my last assignment, was in Turkey. The purpose of this assignment was to train locals in the use of our military tactics. Today they would have called us military advisor or noncombatants. We were working with the militia, not the regular Turkish military. Our orders were to consider the Turkish regulars as unfriendly. Also, that capture was ill-advised as we (Americans) were not supposed to be in this country. Partly the reason for that was our actions in Cyprus.

We were a small group assigned to a larger group of local militia. We worked on teaching tactics, teaching things like hand-to-hand combat, weapons use, surveillance, and counter-surveillance. We were to gain the trust of the local individuals that we were assigned to. This was by far a different type of an assignment for me. I mean, I had classes in teaching some of what we did. But as of yet, I had not done anything like this. I think that was true of most of us. Can't say for sure because it was not discussed, but it sure seemed that way. Add to the mix it was a coed group. That was also new, working

63

in the field with women. While the general argument in the USA has always been women don't belong in combat, my experiences have been that, that is not the case throughout the world. It did pose some interesting problems for me as I was doing the training.

A typical day of training was similar to what we would have done if we were home. Always start with some form of warm-up, usually it was running or swimming, then some type of weapons use, it could be how to field strip a weapon, or how to acquire a target or hand to hand technique. Because of the limited amount of supplies live firing was not very common in training here. Also, included was a modified version of survival, evasion, resistance, and escape training.

The majority of our time was spent on this last form of a training exercise. The Turkish government did not want these rebels trained. Hell, they did not want them alive. It was routine to have active and violent clashes with the Turkish military. It is from this period of time that I have most of my nightmares.

The majority of people have never seen an active, armed combat exchange. It is difficult to understand all that happens in these situations. The emotions that take place during and after. When you have had to fight for your life and the life of others, it is something that you never get over. Once you had one experience you have to fight back all the emotions before you have to go and do it again. You learn very quickly how to shut down your emotions. If you don't, you don't survive!

I have heard others who have been in these situations get asked by friends and family, "What it is like?" The majority of the time they respond with some noncommittal comment. Like "oh it's bad", or "you have no idea" or my favorite "I don't talk about it". The main reason at least for me, is trying to explain what it was like is just not possible. Unless you have walked in my boots, no matter how hard you try, you will not understand.

This does not include all the guilt of living with doing what we did or seeing what we saw. Living with the aftermath of it all. During this time in my life, I was not a Christian. Oh don't get me wrong I believed in God. I was a good Catholic boy. But I did not have the belief in the forgiveness of Christ. I have now accepted God's grace and I know that I am forgiven. But I cannot take back my mistake and therefore still struggle with reconciling what happens next.

I was assigned on point, what would become, my last "training" mission. We had been running into heavy resistance from the military; booby traps, mines, and other devices for the last several days. I was on point because I had been good at finding these things. Besides our US training team, we had about 20 locals that were with us.

We had been out "training" on this day for about 18 hours. While I was on this patrol I found a few booby-traps. A few of the devices had been placed prominently, I think so that we would find them. We occasionally had a few conflicts with small groups of the Turkish military, for lack of a better term. While these conflicts got hot they never escalated enough to require additional support.

You have no idea how extremely difficult it is for me to talk about this. I don't believe in my entire life I've ever talked with anyone, in any detail about this. I've mentioned bits and pieces of this to individuals. I have never tried to fully recant the whole story.

So I was assigned point. I was on point because like I said I was very good at finding tracks and other things. The bottom line - this day, I missed one. That's not an excuse. My job was to protect everybody and I failed miserably. Try to understand that a failure in situations like this means people get hurt and/or die!

We were in light brush in the hill country, strung out fairly well on this trail when it happened. I missed a device. Truth be told it was several devices tied together. It was a device that I didn't realize had been tripped right away. In this situation, my senses were raw from overuse.

I stopped and thought; something was not right. Something just did not "feel" right. It takes a while for the mind to process what is wrong. How quickly I realized what was wrong, is the difference between life and death. That is what happened to me on this day at this moment. I FUBAR'd big time.

The only thing I can remember is that there was, what seemed like, a long delay between when I realized something was wrong and when it went off. It was set specifically on this trail for us, of that I have no doubt. When it blew, it blew my team and our charges apart. Bits and pieces are still only what I remember. Maybe because I don't want to remember.

Carnage was everywhere. Of the 20 to 30 on patrol, only a handful was hurt. The ones who were hurt were hurt badly. I do not know for sure, but I believe many died because of me. Air support for medical evacuation was called. The medics came and started doing their thing. A US corpsmen came to me to evaluate my injuries. I had damage to my lower leg. He grabbed my foot and leg. While twisting them asked me if it hurt. I picked up my weapon and struck him like a club. Not the brightest thing to do but it was a knee-jerk reaction. The barrel hit him in the head and I asked him if that hurt. I guess a dumb question gets a dumb answer.

To this day I don't know what happened to most of the people. I do know why many of them died. They died because I did not do my job. I know that on that day I had one job and I blew it. My mistake cost them their life. That is something that I must live with. That's something that people do not get or understand. People trusted me and because of my mistake, people paid the ultimate price. Sometimes I wish it was me!

I now know I was medevac'd to Naples, Italy. They placed me in an isolation ward. This ward can only be described as a hellhole. Not because it was dirty or not maintained. It was a hellhole because I was isolated. I was isolated not because of any contaminates I had been exposed to. I was in isolation because of what I did and where I had come from. The isolation was a security thing.

I started thinking that somehow the isolation seemed to fit. It was what I deserved. I belonged there. I should not have survived. You hear the people that talk about survivor's remorse, I wonder if that's what I was feeling. I honestly don't know.

One of the hardest things for me was not knowing who on my team survived. Who else was hurt? Who had died? Unfortunately, those are still unanswered questions. There I was in a Naples Hospital. I had at least two surgeries on my leg. I was confined to a bed with nobody around to talk with, or who could talk to me. I would, on rare occasion, have a couple of Navy personnel (at least I thought that's who they were) who would come in and ask stupid questions. They would remind me of keeping classified information classified.

I was able to call home and talk to my mother and father. All they knew was that I was hurt in a hospital in Italy. Of course, that was also all I could tell them. I think my dad figured out that something was up because of the lack of details I could share. I was instructed to say that I was hurt while working on a boiler.

I was in the hospital for about 30 days. I don't think the Navy knew what to do with me. After 30 days I was flown to Germany to another hospital. The hospital gave me the creeps. It was used during WWII by the Nazis for human experiments. Every time I went through a certain area the hairs on the back of my neck would stand up.

I stayed in Germany for a couple of weeks and then it was back to Italy. While in Italy I underwent several additional surgeries to repair the damage to my leg. After a couple of weeks, I was asked to drive an ambulance. The ambulance was to be used for patient transport. While on what was supposed to be a routine transport out to a small base, something went wrong. The person in charge of the transport (I don't know if it was a doctor or a nurse) said something had gone wrong. I was told to get us back to the hospital as quickly as possible.

With the order to hurry I flipped the switch, put the hammer down and moved into the far left lane. On the Autobahn, like the US, the far left lane reserved for the fastest vehicles.

So as I was flying down the Autobahn approaching a toll booth, I was told I did not have to stop and to go through it. I did not slow down much, if at all. I do remember thinking I am glad the outside lane is a lot larger than the other lanes. So as directed, I did not slow down or stop but went right through at high speed. I got to the hospital unloaded the patient and all was fine, or so I thought. As I was parking the ambulance I was met by shore patrol. It seemed that there was a flaw in my information.

When approaching a toll booth you are not required to stop but you are required to slow down to a reasonable speed. No more ambulance driving for me. I was unfit physically to return to my previous duties. Also, I was sure that after what I had done, the SEALs did not want me back. What's the Navy to do with me? At the time I was still in a full leg cast so the Navy sent me back to the fleet.

On a Navy ship, what a civilian would call stairs, the Navy calls a ladder. We call it a ladder because of the steepness of the steps. Within hours of being assigned to a ship, I had broken my cast above the knee. I mean going down the ladders was ok. Trying to bend to come up the ladder could not be done. Additionally, there was the intense heat in the boiler room. If you have ever had a cast on, you know what it feels like when you sweat.

I also believe that the ship I was assigned to did not want anything to do with me. While the sailors in my division were friendly enough, my being so secretive about what happened did not help. When I was told I was being sent back to the fleet as a boiler operator I removed all my other insignias.

Before my release to the fleet, I underwent several meetings and treatments. By the time I returned to the fleet, things in my head did not make sense. While I remembered what happened and what I did. I had conflicting memories. I know that does not make sense. But that's what I remember. I also remember thinking this is what I deserve.

After less than a week on a ship, I was returned to the naval hospital in Virginia. I was told that because of my injuries I was unfit for duty and I was being medically discharged.

11 IT IS FINISHED

My journey of self-exploration has been interesting. When I started, the goal was to simply end my nightmares. I also prayed for answers to some other questions that have always bothered me. Questions like; Which memory is correct? Why can I remember some details but not others? Why can I not remember the number of my BUD's class? Why can I see the face of what I believe are past teammates but cannot remember their names? What happened to me that would cause two memories for the same period in time? Could I have done something different and not have killed all my teammates? Did I do the things I remember? You know, easy questions like these.

Over the years I have spoken with many veterans. It seems that I am not quite as alone as I have always thought. Many of the veterans I have talked to have problems with their memories as well. Maybe it is not to the extent that I have but memory problems all the same.

There is a term I first heard while taking physical rehabilitation class. It seems ironic that I heard it from the wife of a Vietnam veteran. It's called Delayed-onset Post Traumatic Stress Disorder (PTSD). As she told me her story I discovered another purpose for this book.

Her story first: She married her high school sweetheart. After high school, he was drafted into the Army and sent to Vietnam. He did his duty and returned to "the world" and for a while all was fine. He has, to her knowledge, never spoken of his time in the Army. Never spoken of what the war was like or the things he saw or did. He also until recently, had no real emotional issues. That is until recently. It started with simple nightmares. He would awake very abruptly. As she described his nightmares it was like she was speaking about me. As his nightmares got more frequent and violent she tried but could offer any help to him. Eventually, he started going to a counselor. The counselor is the one that diagnosed him with Delayed-onset PTSD. His visits with a counselor, she said, did little to help with his nightmares.

Over the next several weeks of rehab, we talked. We talked about how God had lead me to "accidentally" talk to a counselor at the VA. How He (God) had softened my heart to allow me to get so much from my brief encounter. How my writing down what I could remember of the nightmares had been helping me. She said she wished that there was a book that she could give her husband. "Me too!" I thought.

As I have said, while the nightmares have stopped, many questions remain unanswered. In my quest to try and resolve these unanswered questions I heard about the UDT-SEAL Museum in Fort Pierce, Florida.

On a recent trip to Florida, I included plans to visit this museum. My purpose had a couple of reasons. One thought was it would be interesting to see the origin of naval special operations. The museum is regarded as having a vast library of all things SEAL. Additionally, I thought that exposing myself to the sights and sounds may dislodge some memories to help answer some of my questions.

So on a visit with my family, we went to the museum. I must confess I was a little nervous to enter the museum. The nervousness was because of a couple of things. Would this trip make the nightmares return? Would I find I have been living a lie? Could I finally find out why I have two memories for the same period of my life? And if so, would I like what I found out? These questions are in addition to the earlier questions I have already mentioned.

As we entered and paid the fee we all started into the museum. While my family was checking out the exhibits, I returned to the front counter and asked if either one of the guys there were SEALs. They both were. I explained a little of my background to them and said I was looking for some answers. Their comment surprised me. When I explained my history they responded with "welcome to the club". So while my group was in the museum I went looking into the past.

We started with a computer station that visitors can use to look up past SEALs by name. We checked and my name was not listed. A little disappointing to say the least. My guide said that the computer is not the only records they have. They have hard copies of all the BUD logbooks. The logbooks contain the names of all BUD candidates. The names of the entire class including the ones that quit. So we went in the back and started looking in them. Again no luck on the logbooks.

At this point, my guide started to ask some specific questions. Not in a condescending way, but a "how can I help" kind of way. We began probing into what I could remember. So I told him what I could remember. I included the whole story about how I got into the SEALs. It was during this discussion that my new friend had to chuckle.

As we discussed more of my background I informed him that this period of time has always been a little off. I explained more of what I could remember or thought I could remember. After my Captain's Mast, I was sent to Little Creek VA for my SEAL basic training. I told him I was in Little Creek for training SEALs around 1975.

He indicated that something seemed a little off. He informed me that Little Creek stopped training SEALs in 1971. As we discussed it further he questioned if I was sure about where and when I went. I replied that I am as sure as I can be.

I am sure I was in Little Creek for my BUDs training at a period in time. But, if SEALs no longer trained there what did I do? Part of my memory is receiving my Trident. This new information was not answering anything. Great, just what I needed, more questions. If Little Creek didn't do SEAL training but I remember training in Little Creek what did I do? And if I didn't train as a SEAL what did I train as? Why have I thought that I was a SEAL? Why do I remember being part of SEAL Team 2? More specifically Team 2A as we called ourselves. A visit I thought would answer questions had done the opposite! My new friend at the museum has been very helpful. He totally understood what I was going through. He suggested I contact the Naval Special Warfare Foundation in Washington D.C.

Years ago, when I first started having nightmares and the conflicting memories really started to bother me, I started questioning what the truth could be. Forty years or so earlier, my sister Chris asked me a pointed question. She asked, "If the Government called you today and asked you to do it all over again, knowing what you know of your past, would you serve and do the same thing all over again?" Without hesitation, my answer was, "Absolutely I would". Her response was then let it go and why worry about it now. How does one "let it go", is another question that has always eluded me.

Ten years or so later, another Chris asked me the same question. I gave him the same response. His response was if nothing would change give the conflict to God, accept you are forgiven and move on. Over the years people have made similar comments about accepting forgiveness and moving on. I have always wondered how a person is supposed to do that. I believe that in the process of journaling my nightmares, then writing this book, all the while praying for forgiveness, I am able to finally give this matter to God and leave it with him.

I guess it's time for me to let go of the past. Accept the forgiveness I have been given. I pray that those reading this book will be helped. Either by being encouraged to begin a similar process or by understanding what it is like for others that are fighting similar demons. That is why I have spent the last three years writing this book.

12 MAINTAINING

Just when you think you have everything under control, Bam! I was doing very well keeping my things in a controlled suppression. Or so I thought!

My big day started like any other day. I often joke I get more done before eight o'clock in the morning then a lot of people do all day. This day was no different. Breakfast, meds, a little yard work, an hour or so in my shop. You know a normal routine. Then it happened.

I started getting a little light-headed. Then a feeling that something is not right. All my vital signs were normal. But I felt like I was dying. My arms and legs were so heavy. It was like they were wrapped with lead. I could not move them. I didn't have the strength to lift them. My breathing was slowing. My heart rate was going down. It did not look good. Everyone around me said it was like I was having a stroke. I felt like I was having another stroke. I had the thought that this was it. I would be with Jesus this morning. While I was glad, I was also sad.

I was on the phone with my daughter and she knew something was wrong. She asked if I wanted her to call an ambulance. I think she was surprised when I said yes. The ambulance came and I got a free ride to the hospital emergency room. Ok, I know it's not free. By the time I got to the hospital I was unable to speak clearly enough to make myself understood. I still could not seem to move very well. The hospital started testing and determined that it was not a stroke. Yay team!

We have no idea for sure what happened but it definitely was not a stroke. I was admitted for observation. By 1900 hours or so my speech started to return. Not fully but enough to talk and be understood. My wife said that she could understand me but it didn't sound like me. By 2100 hours I was pretty much back to normal.

The next day in the hospital, I was up shaving when I got the light-headed feeling again. This one was a little different. I was also getting very hot and starting to sweat. I don't mean a little wet. No, I was wet like I just got out of a pool. When they tried to run the EKG the leads would not stick because I was so wet with sweat.

EKG was normal! All the other vitals were normal. As they were trying to figure out was going on with me my nurse suggested they check my blood sugar. My blood sugar had dropped dangerously low. So low they didn't believe their results. They grabbed another glucometer and checked it again. The second reading was lower than the first.

They gave me something to get my sugar levels up and I started to return to normal. The doctors had me scheduled for a heart stress test so off I went. Everything was fine. During the test, however, I had my first (for lack of a better term) flashback.

I was lying there resting. Just kind of dozing when it hit. I was back in Turkey right after the explosion. I could see everything in full color. I could taste it. I could smell it. I could hear it. I literally jump off the gurney. Almost pulled the IV out. My nurse came running in. Did I mention that I was on a heart monitor?

Like most people I have tracked what can cause episodes. Looking back on the last couple of days, none of my known triggers had been triggered. In the past my method to get through an episode was to repeat to myself three things - "I am home, I am safe and Jesus loves me". The other thing I have done was to start writing down these dreams/flashbacks. At first, nothing was helping!

After the episode while having my stress test I had another one while they were taking me back to my room. Exactly the same as the last one. It seemed that any time I tried to quiet myself BAM I would have another flashback. Always the same place and time.

As far back as I can remember these dreams were just that, dreams. I mean they only happened after I was asleep. Now I was having them while I was awake. Also in the past, I would be at different locations or different points at the same event. Now I keep coming back to the same point.

I was back on my last mission. When this new round of episodes started to happen, it seemed to me that was in the thick of it back to the moment right after the explosion. Not in a hospital, present day, but back in the field. It takes a little while for my brain to realize I was in a hospital. Before the realization hit I would be in a panic. Panic because I am under attack; I have to get back in the fight; the pain in my leg is intense; I must calm down. Where are my weapons? Where is the threat and how can I neutralize it? All of these things flash through my mind seemingly at once.

While my three phrases helped they did not remove the feeling. They also did not remove the smells or the tastes. Nor the sense of being under attack. Or the issue of my failure! I feel like a caged animal looking to explode at the first target that I come across. For me, this is the scariest thing. This feeling of not being in control. Then the realization hits me and I wonder, did I hurt anyone before I realized I was not under attack? Will I attack someone next time? What if somebody touches me thinking they were, trying to help me? Would I interpret that as a threat? And retaliate before I realize what was going on?

It took a few weeks for me to remember what started this whole thing with writing this book. For me to remember how much journaling helped me before. So I again started writing down what I could remember from the latest flashbacks. As I started trying to remember details of the events and write them down, the frequency of those events started getting further and further apart. And then, thank God, they stopped.

It never ceases to amaze me the inconspicuous ways that God use to get our attention. Ok, sometimes not so inconspicuous. It brings to great clarity the verse that directs us "to be still and know that I am God", Proverbs 46:10a.

EPILOGUE

Before I started the process of writing this book a typical week for me was one of the unknown. I was always worried and/or fearful. My concern was "Is this the week that I am not going to keep my anger under control and end up seriously hurting someone?" I say this because in the past when I lost control, usually one of two things would happen; 1) someone ended up in the hospital or 2) I diverted the anger by driving my fist into a wall. The scary part for me was sometime I wanted it to be people, fortunately, it was not often. But once is enough to keep me scared!

Another area I worried about was the nightmares themselves. When I woke up I was caught between sleep, the dream, and not being fully aware of the fact that I was dreaming. During these times of transition, I would often orally recite "it's ok", "I'm home", or, "I'm safe no one is trying to kill me". Here is an example while home on leave, visiting my parents at their home in Michigan. My mother decided to tiptoe into the room I was sleeping in. As she neared the bed, while mostly asleep, I grasped her by the neck chocking her while my other hand was coming down to break her neck. I woke up in time to not kill her but not in time to not strike. She was alright but had a sore neck for a long time.

I know some people will read the above statement and chuckle. They may disregard the statement or lessen the meaning by thinking "it's not as bad as all that". Please believe me if you have never been there then you have no reference point. This is one of the reasons, I believe, most veterans don't tell their story.

We see the reaction in your eyes, in your stance, even in the rest of your body language. Also when I first started telling my story for this book I found out that I would often mix the events together. I cannot to this day begin to tell you why.

Another thing writing this book has done for me is that it has brought a better clarity into my life about my Lord and Savior. Before you get all "he is one of those", let me explain. Being a follower of Christ has had a profound impact on my life. Read Final Inspection, inside front cover. I truly believe that one day we will all have a final inspection. Because of my belief in Christ, the last line will apply to me. If you are not a Christ-follower my hope is that because of what you have read you will take a closer look. Yes, I have given up things. Things like the constant guilt for what I had to do while at work. Even the things I have had to do since I got out.

When Christ took these things from me it was not like "poof" they're gone. Although I do know people that He has done it that way for. My experience has been tiny changes that remove big issues, a little at a time. But I can say with confidence I am more at peace with each passing day.

APPENDIX

Forgiveness

As I mentioned in the book; I was able to find peace through accepting that God loves me and has forgiven me. If you are looking for a relationship with God, along with His peace and forgiveness, this prayer may help:

"Dear God, I know that I am a sinner and there is nothing that I can do to save myself. I confess my complete helplessness to forgive my own sin. At this moment I trust Christ alone as the One who bore my sin when He died on the cross. I believe that because Jesus died for my sin, I am totally forgiven. I thank you that Christ was raised from the dead as a guarantee of my own resurrection. As best as I can, I now transfer my trust to Him. I am grateful that He has promised to receive me despite my many sins and failures. Father, I take you at your word. Thank you for the assurance that You will walk with me through my toughest days. Thank you for hearing this prayer. In Jesus' Name. Amen."

Hope

Here are a few scriptures that have helped me and may help you on your journey:

Romans 10:9-10 New Living Translation (NLT)

[9] If you openly declare that Jesus is Lord and believe in your heart that God raised him from the dead, you will be saved. [10] For it is by believing in your heart that you are made right with God, and it is by openly declaring your faith that you are saved.

Isaiah 43:25 New Living Translation (NLT)

[25] "I—yes, I alone—will blot out your sins for my own sake
   and will never think of them again.

Micah 7:18-19 New Living Translation (NLT)

[18] Where is another God like you,
   who pardons the guilt of the remnant,
   overlooking the sins of his special people?
You will not stay angry with your people forever,
   because you delight in showing unfailing love.
[19] Once again you will have compassion on us.
   You will trample our sins under your feet
   and throw them into the depths of the ocean!

Ephesians 1:7-8 New Living Translation (NLT)

[7] He is so rich in kindness and grace that he purchased our freedom with the blood of his Son and forgave our sins. [8] He has showered his kindness on us, along with all wisdom and understanding.

Colossians 1:13-14 New Living Translation (NLT)

[13] For he has rescued us from the kingdom of darkness and transferred us into the Kingdom of his dear Son, [14] who purchased our freedom and forgave our sins.

1 John 1:9 New Living Translation (NLT)

[9] But if we confess our sins to him, he is faithful and just to forgive us our sins and to cleanse us from all wickedness.

Come Visit My Grave

By Jim Rolfes

I am a Veteran under the sod.

I'm in good company, I'm up here with God.

Come to my grave and visit me.

I gave my life so you could be free.

Today is Memorial Day throughout this great land.

There's Avenues of Flags, Parades and Bands.

I can hear music, the firing squads and taps.

Here come my comrades, the Legionnaires, the Blue caps.

One of them just put a flag on my stone.

Someday he'll have one of his own.

Some think of this day as just a day free of toil.

While others are busy working the soil.

They say they have plans, other things to do.

Don't put us aside as you would an old shoe.

Come visit my grave in this cemetery so clean.

This is what Memorial Day means.

There are many of us lying in wakeless sleep.

In cemeteries of green and oceans of deep.

It's sad that for many who fought so brave.

No one comes to visit their grave.

They died so you could have one whole year free.

Now can't you save this one Day for me?

There are soldiers, sailors, airmen up here.

Who went into battle despite of their fear.

I've been talking up here to all of those men.

If they had to do it over, they'd do it again.

Look, someone is coming to visit my grave.

It's my Family, for them my life I gave.

My wife, I remember our last embrace.

As I left the tears streamed down your face.

I think you knew the day I was shipped out.

I wouldn't return, your life would be turned about.

There's my daughter that I used to hold.

Can it be that you're nearly twenty years old?

Next month is to be your wedding day.

I wish I could be there to give you away.

My son's here too, Dad's little man.

Always love your Country, do for it what you can.

There is one thing that really did bother.

Is seeing you grow up without the aid of your father.

I wish you could all hear me from up above.

That's a father's best gift to his children is love.

And what better way to prove my love to the end.

Is that a man lay down his life for his friends.

I see it's time for you to go home.

Your visit made it easier to remain here alone.

Don't cry honey, you look too sad.

Our children are free, you should be so glad.

Daughter, thanks for the bouquet so cute.

Thank you son for that sharp salute.

Come again, I forgot, you can't hear me from up here.

But I know you'll come visit me again next year.

I hope all veterans are treated this way.

On this day to remember, Memorial Day.

Journal

This next part might not sound like the best idea to you. Trust me, I wanted no parts of it myself. Anyone who knows me can tell you that journaling was the last thing I ever wanted to do. I did not even take notes during college or in my Bible study classes. But once I decided to finally give it a try, it changed my life. On the following pages there is space for you to use however you see fit. If you are experiencing nightmares you may began to write them down. Maybe jot down memories or things you want to recall. Tell your story the best way that works for you. For me, writing has been healing, I hope for you it can be the same.

Made in the USA
Middletown, DE
14 September 2019